Got Calls?

Conference Calls Note-Taking Composition

Alicia "WATERS"

GOT CALLS?

For ordering, booking, permission, or questions, contact the author.
www.amazon.com/author/alicianwaters
www.anwempires@gmail.com

ISBN:9781077277038

Printed in the United States of America by Kindle Direct Publishing

GOT CALLS?

Call Notes:

Call Notes:

Call Notes:

Call Notes:

Call Notes:

Call Notes:

Call Notes:

Call Notes:

Call Notes:

Call Notes:

Call Notes:

Call Notes:

Call Notes:

Call Notes:

Call Notes:

GOT CALLS?

Call Notes:

Call Notes:

.

Call Notes:

Call Notes:

Call Notes:

Call Notes:

GOT CALLS?

Call Notes:

Call Notes:

Call Notes:

Call Notes:

Call Notes:

Call Notes:

Call Notes:

Call Notes:

Call Notes:

Call Notes:

Call Notes:

Call Notes:

Call Notes:

Call Notes:

Call Notes:

Call Notes:

Call Notes:

GOT CALLS?

Call Notes:

Call Notes:

Call Notes:

Call Notes:

Call Notes:

Call Notes:

Call Notes:

Call Notes:

Call Notes:

Call Notes:

Call Notes:

Call Notes:

Call Notes:

Call Notes:

Call Notes:

Call Notes:

Call Notes:

Call Notes:

Call Notes:

GOT CALLS?

Call Notes:

Call Notes:

Call Notes:

Call Notes:

Call Notes:

Call Notes:

Call Notes:

Call Notes:

Call Notes:

Call Notes:

Call Notes:

Call Notes:

Call Notes:

Call Notes:

GOT CALLS?

Call Notes:

Call Notes:

Call Notes:

Call Notes:

Call Notes:

Call Notes:

.

Call Notes:

Call Notes:

Call Notes:

Call Notes:

Call Notes:

Call Notes:

Call Notes:

Call Notes:

GOT CALLS?

Call Notes:

Call Notes:

Call Notes:

Call Notes:

Call Notes:

Call Notes:

Call Notes:

Call Notes:

GOT CALLS?

Call Notes:

Call Notes:

Call Notes:

Call Notes:

Related Resource on Amazon

Noteworthy: (Freestyle Writing & Note Taking Composition)

Visit the Author's Amazon Page
www.amazon.com/author/alicianwaters

To Book the Author for
Speaking Engagements
Email: anwempires@gmail.com

If you enjoyed this resource, please feel free to leave a positive review on Amazon.

Thanks & Blessings

GOT CALLS?

www.ingramcontent.com/pod-product-compliance
Lightning Source LLC
Chambersburg PA
CBHW080940170526
45158CB00008B/2322